Table of Contents

Chevron Tiles,
page 18

Royal Diamonds,
page 36

Asian Reflections Pillows,
page 8

HOUSE of
WHITE
BIRCHES
PUBLISHERS
SINCE 1947

String Quilting Today is published by DRG, 306 East Parr Road, Berne, IN 46711. Printed in USA. Copyright © 2011 DRG. All rights reserved. This publication may not be reproduced in part or in whole without written permission from the publisher.

RETAIL STORES: If you would like to carry this pattern book or any other DRG publications, visit DRGwholesale.com.

Every effort has been made to ensure that the instructions in this pattern book are complete and accurate. We cannot, however, take responsibility for human error, typographical mistakes or variations in individual work. Please visit ClotildeCustomerCare.com to check for pattern updates.

ISBN: 978-1-59217-327-3
2 3 4 5 6 7 8 9

Strings & Things

Making string-pieced quilts is a good way to use small pieces or "strings" left over from other projects. Thrifty quilters save small scraps and are always looking for ways to use them in a quilt. String piecing makes use of those pieces to create fun finished quilts.

Strings

In quilting parlance "strings" are long narrow pieces of fabric. They may be any width from 1" to 3" wide, or slightly wider, by whatever length is left from another project or larger piece of fabric.

They can be cut straight or at an angle, according to what you want your finished quilt to look like. Using straight strings will present a planned look, while strings of various widths and angles will present a scrappy look. Use scraps left over from other fabric projects and leftover binding, sashing or blocks from other quilting projects.

Sorting Your Strings

The strings may be sorted into color families or color combinations that you want to use for your quilt. Those fabrics with several colors should be sorted according to the predominate color. These pieces can give your quilt a little extra interest. On the other hand, you may use an assortment of strings that go well together. This will give you a scrappy look. Many of the quilts in this book use strings of the same color family to create a particular look in the block. Others use a variety of colors to blend with background or setting pieces.

Foundation Piecing

A foundation is used when strings of varying widths are used to create the string-pieced units or pieces. This provides stability to pieces that may have been cut on the bias or have no straight edges.

Foundation pieces may be cut from paper, muslin or "wonder fabric,"—"I wonder why I bought that?!" You can even recycle worn bed sheets. Don't try to use dark foundation pieces under light-color fabric because the dark color may show through.

Paper used as foundations should be removed before the quilt is finished. Fabric foundations are left on and are a permanent part of the quilt, creating a heavier finished product.

String Strip Sets

String strip sets are made by joining several strings together along the length of the string or strip.

The string strips can be controlled—that is, all of the strings can be trimmed to the same length to create a pieced strip of the desired height.

Uncontrolled string strip sets are made from strings of various sizes to create a set of the desired height. The block pieces are then cut from the template as if it were a single fabric.

Around a Square

Strings can also be pieced around a center patch. That patch could be a square, triangle, rectangle or other shape. Usually the strings are all the same size, but not always. The only requirement when using blocks made using varying-width strings is that all blocks finish at the same size so they can be pieced together.

The Log Cabin block is the primary pattern that uses this technique. The bed runner Chevron Tiles (page 18) uses a Chevron block with log strings of varying widths. ❖

Meet the Designer

Connie Ewbank learned to embroider when she was in grade school and crochet when she was in high school. She has tried and enjoyed many different crafts. She made her first quilt for her sister, who was expecting a baby. She has been making quilts ever since.

Connie owned a quilt and cross-stitch shop—Quilt N Stitch—in St. Louis, Mo., for 12 years. The shop offered lots of classes, many of them taught from designs created at the shop. Connie began to publish these designs in pattern and book form. She also purchased a separate counted cross-stitch shop where she designed and taught classes.

In the early fall of 2004, Connie closed both shops and moved to the Baton Rouge, La., area. She has continued to teach and design patterns for both quilting and counted cross-stitch. She publishes her cross-stitch designs under the name of Butterfly Stitches.

Teaching has taken Connie to many places around the Missouri, Ohio, Illinois and Kansas areas, and as far away as Monterrey, Mexico. Since moving to Louisiana, she has expanded her teaching area to include Mississippi, Florida and North Carolina. Connie has taught at local quilt guilds, local and regional Embroiderers' Guild of America (EGA) meetings, local American Needlepoint Guild (ANG) meetings, and is currently a Gulf States Quilting Association circuit teacher.

Connie lives in Denham Springs, La., with her two cats. She says her home has become her workshop for designing, sewing and maintaining her pattern company.

Acknowledgements

Several quilts in this book were professionally machine-quilted by Carol Hilton on her longarm machine.

Thank you, Carol, for making time in your busy schedule to quilt the Diamond Holiday, Summer Garden, Play Ball!, Autumn Equinox, Chevron Tiles and Royal Diamonds quilts. They are beautiful.

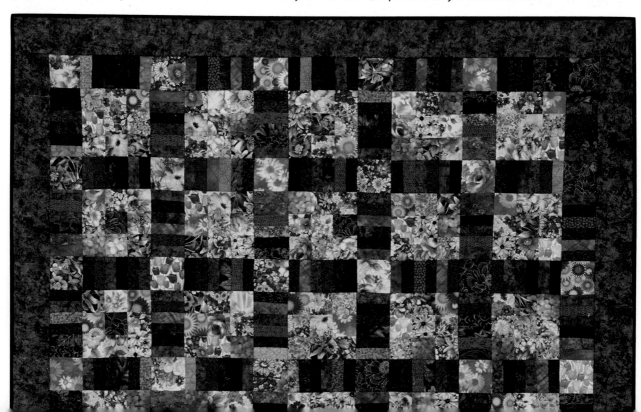

Market Time Table Runner

Make this quick and easy table runner with fruit and veggie fabrics, or a variety of other theme fabrics.

Project Specifications
Skill Level: Beginner
Runner Size: 48" x 20"

Materials
- Assorted scraps or 7½"-long strings of varied-width food-theme fabrics
- ¾ yard green tonal
- Batting 56" x 28"
- Backing 56" x 28"
- Neutral-color all-purpose thread
- Invisible thread
- Quilting thread
- Basic sewing tools and supplies

Cutting
1. Cut a variety of fabric strings 7½" or longer and in varying widths from assorted food-theme fabrics for A. **Note:** *If using scraps, trim to make all the strings a uniform length of 7½". Strings may range in width, depending on the width of your scraps. Since the string unit is trimmed after piecing, it doesn't matter how wide they are as long as they are the same length along the entire string unit.*

2. Cut four 2½" by fabric width strips green tonal. Join strips on short ends to make one strip; press seams open. Subcut strip into three 44½" B strips.

3. Cut one 2½" by fabric width strip green tonal; subcut strip into two 2½" x 20½" C strips.

4. Cut four 2¼" by fabric width strips green tonal for binding.

Completing the Runner

1. Join the A strings on the 7½" edges to make a string unit at least 44½" long as shown in Figure 1; press seams in one direction.

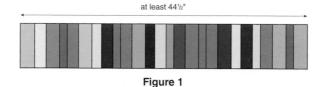

at least 44½"

Figure 1

2. Trim the string unit made in step 1 as necessary to make one 7½" x 44½" A unit, referring to Figure 2. *Note: If all A strings were trimmed to 7½" in length, height of the unit should not have to be trimmed.*

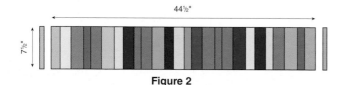

44½"

7½"

Figure 2

3. Repeat steps 1 and 2 to make a second A unit.

4. Join the two A units with the three B strips, beginning and ending with a B strip, referring to the Placement Diagram; press seams toward B strips.

5. Sew a C strip to each short end of the A-B unit to complete the pieced top; press seams toward C strips.

Finishing

1. Press runner top on both sides; check for proper seam pressing and trim all loose threads.

2. Sandwich batting between the stitched top and the backing piece; pin or baste layers together to hold. Quilt as desired by hand or machine. *Note: The quilt shown was randomly machine-quilted in the ditch of seams on the A units using invisible thread in the top of the machine and ¼" from seams on B and C strips using thread to match fabrics.*

3. When quilting is complete, trim batting and backing fabric even with raw edges of runner top.

4. Join binding strips on short ends with diagonal seams as shown in Figure 3 to make one long strip; trim seams to ¼" and press seams open.

¼"

Figure 3

5. Fold the binding strip with wrong sides together along length; press.

6. Sew binding to runner top edges, mitering corners and overlapping ends. Fold binding to the back side and stitch in place to finish. ❖

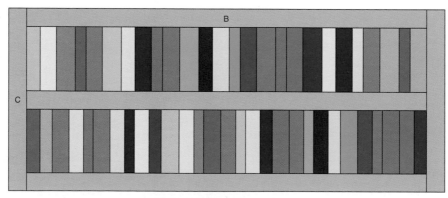

Market Time Table Runner
Placement Diagram 48" x 20"

Asian Reflection Pillows

Choose a fabric you really like, and then choose four or five fabrics that blend with it. Make a fun pillow or two for your home or make them as gifts.

Project Specifications
Skill Level: Confident Beginner
Pillow Size: 18" x 18"
Block Size: 7" x 7"
Number of Blocks: 4 per pillow

Materials
- 10–12 scrap strings 20" or longer to coordinate with focus fabric
- 1 fat quarter black-with-gold dot
- 1 fat quarter black solid
- ½ yard green-with-gold metallic print
- 1 yard black Asian print (focus fabric)
- 2 batting squares 22" x 22"
- 2 backing squares 22" x 22"
- Black all-purpose thread
- Black machine-quilting thread
- 2 (18" x 18") square pillow forms
- Template material
- Basic sewing tools and supplies

Cutting
1. Trim scrap string pieces in varying widths as desired.

2. Cut two 2½" x 21" strips green-with-gold metallic print; subcut strips into two 7½" G and two 9½" H strips.

3. Cut two 2½" x 21" strips black-with-gold dot; subcut strips into two 7½" I and two 9½" J strips.

4. Cut four 2½" x 21" strips black solid; trim strips to make two 14½" K strips and two 18½" L strips.

5. Cut one 18½" by fabric width strip black Asian print; subcut strip into two 18½" squares for pillow backs.

6. Prepare templates for A/C/E and B/D/F using patterns given; mark centers. Cut all except the string-set pieces as directed on patterns; mark the center of each piece.

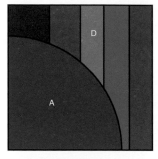

Black A/D Curve
7" x 7" Block
Make 2

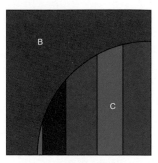

Black B/C Curve
7" x 7" Block
Make 2

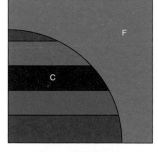

Green C/F Curve
7" x 7" Block
Make 2

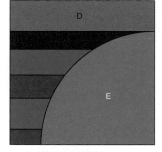

Green E/D Curve
7" x 7" Block
Make 2

Completing the Black Curve Blocks
1. Join the strings along lengths to make a string set at least 8" x 20"; press seams in one direction. Repeat to make a second string set.

2. Cut the C and D pieces from the string sets using templates and referring to Figure 1 for positioning of templates on strings; mark the center of each piece. Set aside two each C and D pieces for Green Curve blocks.

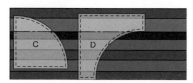

Figure 1

3. Select one each C and B piece; pin right sides together, matching center marks as shown in Figure 2.

Figure 2

4. Match and pin ends of pieces together as shown in Figure 3.

Figure 3

5. Stitch pieces together, adjusting pieces as you stitch to create a flat seam as shown in Figure 4.

Figure 4

6. Clip into seam as necessary referring to Figure 5.

Figure 5

7. Press the stitched unit flat to complete one Black B/C Curve block.

8. Repeat steps 3–7 to complete a second Black B/C Curve block.

9. Repeat steps 3–8 with the A and D pieces to complete two Black A/D Curve blocks referring to Figure 6.

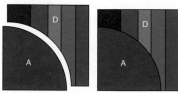

Figure 6

Completing the Green Curve Blocks

1. Using C pieces set aside earlier and F pieces, join one of each piece as in steps 3–8 for Completing the Black Curve Blocks to complete two Green C/F Curve blocks as shown in Figure 7.

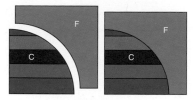

Figure 7

2. Using D pieces set aside earlier and E pieces, join one of each piece as in steps 3–8 for Completing the Black Curve Blocks to complete two Green D/E Curve blocks as shown in Figure 8.

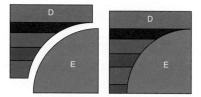

Figure 8

Completing the Black Pillow Top

1. Select one each Black A/D and Black B/C Curve blocks and arrange in two rows of two blocks each as shown in Figure 9; join in rows. Press seams in opposite directions. Join the rows to complete the black pillow center; press seam in one direction.

Black Pieced Pillow Center

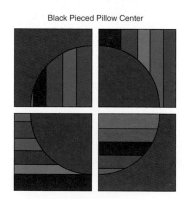

Figure 9

2. Join one each G and I strip on the short ends to make a G-I strip; press seams open. Repeat to make a second G-I strip.

3. Repeat step 2 with H and J to complete two H-J strips.

4. Sew the G-I strips to opposite sides and H-I strips to the remaining sides of the black pillow center as shown in Figure 10 to complete the black pillow top.

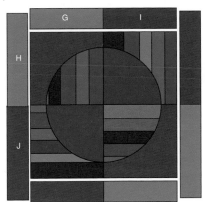

Figure 10

Completing the Green Pillow Top

1. Select two each Green C/F Curve and Green D/E Curve blocks and arrange in two rows of two blocks as shown in Figure 11; join in rows. Press seams in opposite directions. Join the rows to complete the green pillow center; press seam in one direction.

Green Pieced Pillow Center

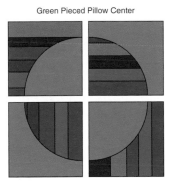

Figure 11

2. Referring to the Placement Diagram, sew a K strip to opposite sides and L strips to the remaining sides of the green pillow center to complete the green pillow top; press seams toward K and L strips.

Finishing

1. Press each pillow top on both sides; check for proper seam pressing and trim all loose threads.

2. Sandwich a batting square between one pillow top and a backing square; pin or baste layers together to hold. Quilt as desired by hand or machine. ***Note:*** *The sample pillows were machine-quilted in the ditch of seams using black thread.*

3. When quilting is complete, trim batting and backing fabric even with raw edges of the pillow top.

4. Repeat steps 1–3 with the second pillow top.

5. Place an Asian print pillow-back square right sides together with a quilted pillow top; stitch all around, leaving a 10" opening on one side. Secure stitching at beginning and end of seam.

Black Asian Reflection Pillow
Placement Diagram 18" x 18"

6. Trim corners; turn right side out through the opening. Press edges flat.

7. Turn in the ¼" seam allowance on each open edge and press.

8. Insert pillow form through opening.

9. Hand-stitch the pressed open edges together to finish as shown in Figure 12.

10. Repeat steps 5–9 to complete the second pillow. ❖

Figure 12

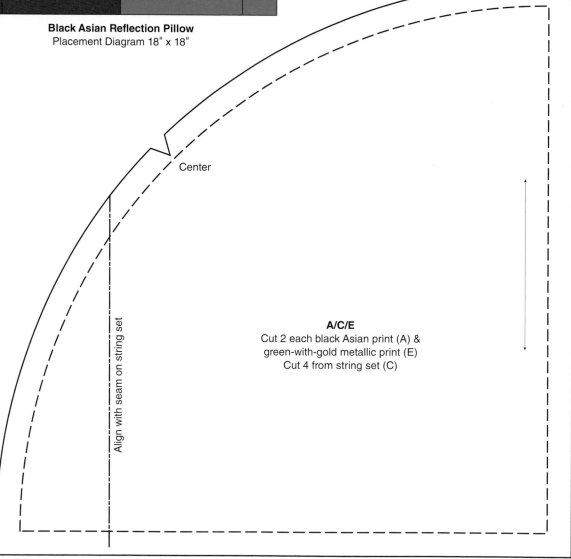

Center

Align with seam on string set

A/C/E
Cut 2 each black Asian print (A) &
green-with-gold metallic print (E)
Cut 4 from string set (C)

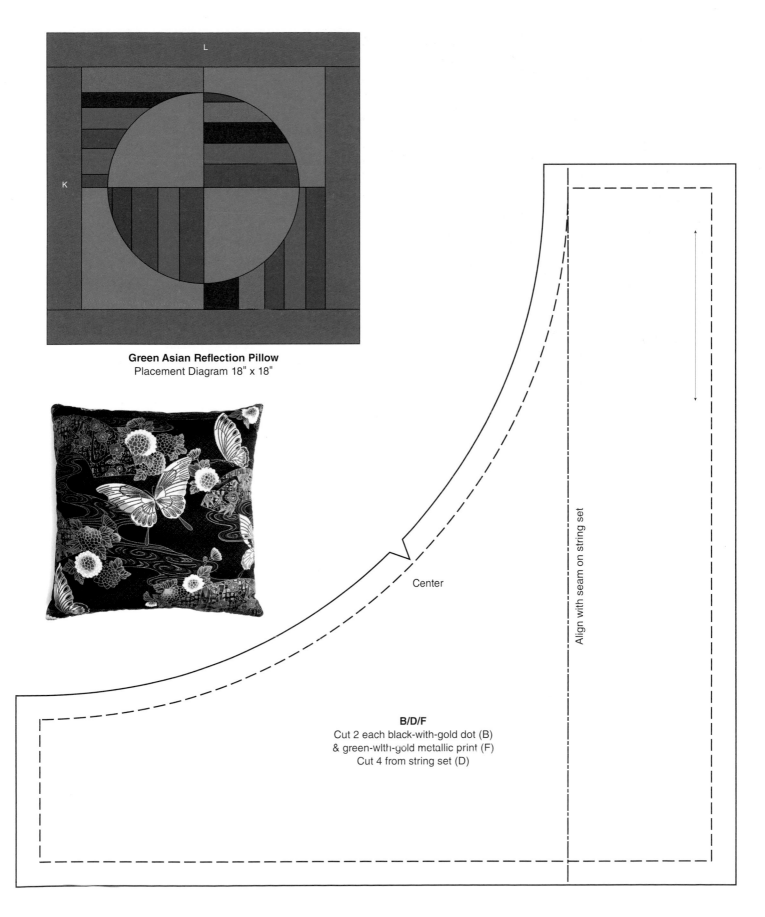

Green Asian Reflection Pillow
Placement Diagram 18" x 18"

Align with seam on string set

Center

B/D/F
Cut 2 each black-with-gold dot (B)
& green-with-gold metallic print (F)
Cut 4 from string set (D)

Sweet Dolly Quilt

What little girl wouldn't love having a special quilt for her dolly? This one is especially sweet, and can be made with or without the little flowers.

Project Specifications
Skill Level: Beginner
Quilt Size: 22" x 28"
Block Size: 6" x 6"
Number of Blocks: 12

Materials
- ¼ yard each 4–6 different pastel floral prints
- ⅜ yard yellow tonal
- ⅝ yard blue mottled
- Batting 30" x 36"
- Backing 30" x 36"
- Neutral-color all-purpose thread
- Invisible thread
- Quilting thread
- Fabric glue stick
- Freezer paper
- Template material
- Basic sewing tools and supplies

Cutting
1. Cut one 6⅞" by fabric width strip yellow tonal; subcut strip into six 6⅞" squares. Cut each square in half on one diagonal to make a total of 12 A triangles as shown in Figure 1.

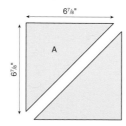

Figure 1

2. Cut two strings from each pastel floral print, varying widths between 1½"–2" for B.

3. Cut two 2½" x 24½" C strips and two 2½" x 22½" D strips blue mottled.

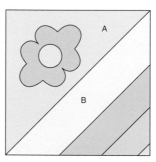

String Triangle
6" x 6" Block
Make 12

4. Cut three 2¼" by fabric width strips blue mottled for binding.

5. Trace appliqué shapes onto the paper side of freezer paper as directed on pattern for number to cut; cut out shapes on traced lines.

6. Iron the freezer-paper shapes with waxy side down on the wrong side of the appliqué fabrics; cut out shapes. Remove freezer paper. ***Note:*** *Freezer-paper shapes are being used here to make easy-to-use stick-on patterns for cutting pieces.*

Completing the Blocks
1. Select and join B strings to make two string sets that are at least 5" wide by fabric width; press seams in one direction.

2. Prepare template for B using pattern given. Place the template on the string sets and cut 12 B triangles as shown in Figure 2.

Figure 2

3. Join one each A and B triangle as shown in Figure 3 to complete an A-B unit; press seam toward B. Repeat to complete a total of 12 A-B units.

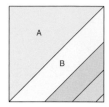

Figure 3

4. Apply fabric glue to the wrong side of a flower and a flower center piece, and place the flower and then the center on the A area of one A-B unit referring to the block drawing for positioning; reposition as necessary.

5. When satisfied with positioning of motif, stitch around each shape using invisible thread in the top of the machine to complete one String Triangle block.

6. Repeat steps 4 and 5 with remaining flower motifs and A-B units to complete a total of 12 String Triangle blocks.

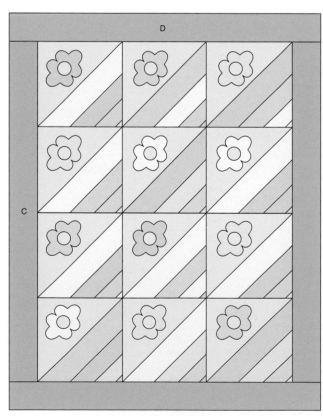

Sweet Dolly Quilt
Placement Diagram 22" x 28"

Piecing the Top

1. Select and join three String Triangle blocks to make a row as shown in Figure 4; press seams toward the left. Repeat to make a total of four rows, pressing seams in two of the rows toward the left and two toward the right.

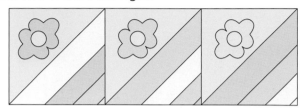

Figure 4

2. Join the rows, alternating the seam pressing in rows, to complete the pieced center; press seams in one direction.

3. Sew C strips to opposite long sides and D strips to the top and bottom of the pieced center to complete the quilt top; press seams toward C and D strips.

Finishing

1. Press quilt top on both sides; check for proper seam pressing and trim all loose threads.

2. Sandwich batting between the stitched top and the backing piece; pin or baste layers together to hold. Quilt as desired by hand or machine. *Note: The quilt shown was machine-quilted in the ditch of seams and around appliqué pieces using invisible thread in the top of the machine.*

3. When quilting is complete, trim batting and backing fabric even with raw edges of quilt top.

4. Join binding strips on short ends with diagonal seams as shown in Figure 5 to make one long strip; trim seams to ¼" and press seams open.

Figure 5

5. Fold the binding strip with wrong sides together along length; press.

6. Sew binding to quilt top edges, mitering corners and overlapping ends. Fold binding to the back side and stitch in place to finish. ❖

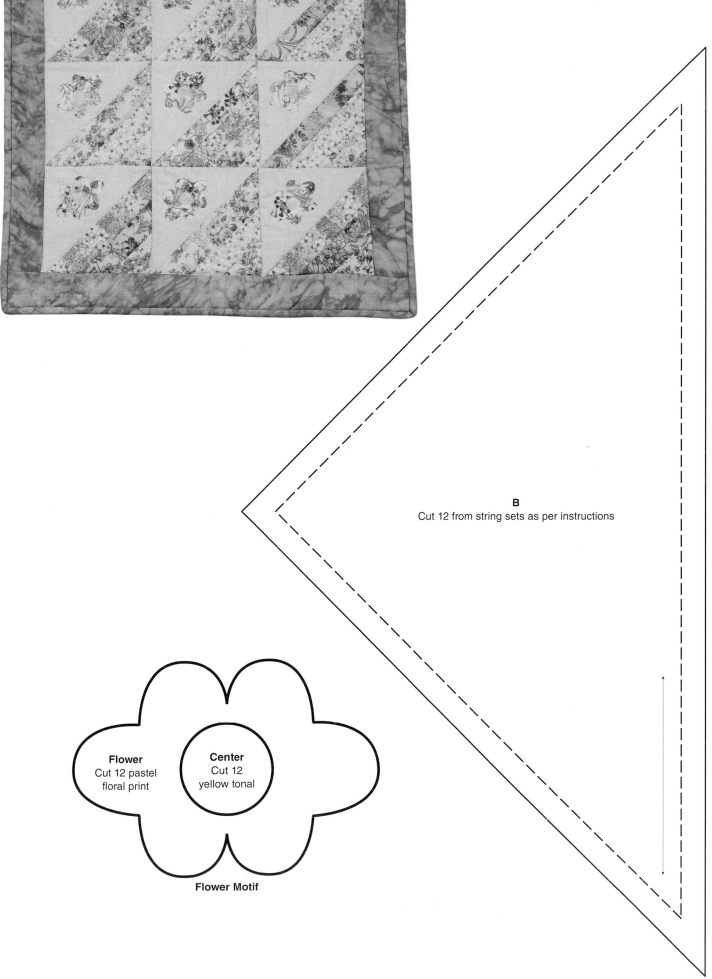

B
Cut 12 from string sets as per instructions

Flower
Cut 12 pastel
floral print

Center
Cut 12
yellow tonal

Flower Motif

Chevron Tiles

A bed runner can be decorative, but also helps to keep your feet warm on cold winter nights. Choose colors to match or contrast with your bedroom to add personality to the room.

Project Notes

To make 20 blocks, you will need 20 of each size piece used in the blocks. The bed runner will be more interesting if you use a variety of fabrics for each piece, making the finished blocks all look different. This is especially true for the A squares, since four of these will be stitched together in the four-block units. Light and dark fabrics should be distributed throughout the blocks.

Note that the strings used to make the logs are not all the same width.

Project Specifications

Skill Level: Beginner
Runner Size: 81" x 21"
Block Size: 7½" x 7½"
Number of Blocks: 20

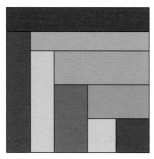

Chevron
7½" x 7½" Block
Make 20

Materials

- Fat quarters of 10–12 assorted coordinating batiks in colors from light to dark
- 1⅛ yards batik in coordinating dark color
- Batting 89" x 29"
- Backing 89" x 29"
- Neutral-color all-purpose thread
- Quilting thread
- Basic sewing tools and supplies

Cutting

1. Cut one 1½" x 21" strip from each batik fat quarter; subcut strips into a total of (20) 6¾" G strips. *Note: Be sure to cut strips from all fabrics to create a variety in the completed blocks.*

2. Cut two 1¾" x 21" strips from each batik fat quarter; subcut strips into a total of 20 each 5¾" F, 6¾" H and 8" I strips.

3. Cut two 2¼" x 21" strips from each batik fat quarter; subcut strips into a total of 20 each of the following sizes: 2¼" A, 2" B, 3¾" C, 4" D and 5½" E.

4. Cut five 3½" by fabric width strips coordinating dark-color batik; subcut one strip into two 3½" x 21½" K. Set aside remaining strips for J border strips.

5. Cut six 2½" by fabric width strips coordinating dark-color batik for binding.

Completing the Blocks

1. Select one of each size lettered piece from A–I for one block.

2. Lay pieces out on a flat surface in alphabetical order referring to Figure 1 to check for color positioning.

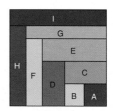

Figure 1

3. To complete one Chevron block using the arranged pieces, sew A to B; press seam toward B.

4. Sew C to the A-B unit; press seam toward C.

5. Continue to add pieces to the A-B-C unit in alphabetical order as arranged in Figure 1 to complete one Chevron block, pressing seams toward the pieces as added.

20

6. Repeat steps 1–5 to complete a total of 20 Chevron blocks.

Completing the Top

1. Select four Chevron blocks. Arrange blocks in two rows of two blocks each with A pieces in the center as shown in Figure 2.

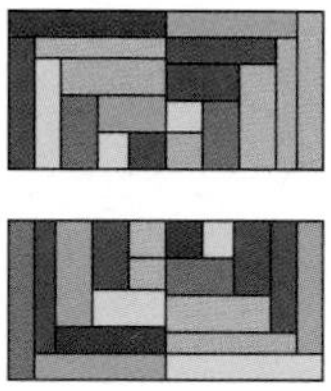

Figure 2

2. Join the blocks as arranged to make two rows; press seams to one side.

3. Join the rows to complete a four-block unit as shown in Figure 3; press seam to one side.

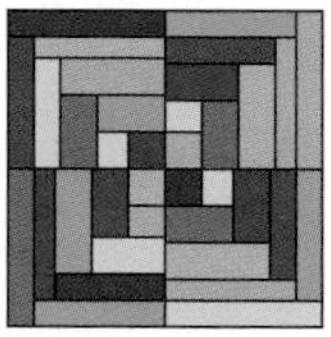

Figure 3

4. Repeat steps 1–3 to complete a total of five four-block units.

5. Join the four-block units, alternating orientation of seam allowance pressing, to complete the pieced center; press seams in one direction.

6. Join the J strips on short ends to make a long strip; press seams open. Subcut strip into two 75½" J strips.

7. Sew J strips to opposite long sides and K strips to the short ends of the pieced center to complete the runner top; press seams toward J and K strips.

Finishing

1. Press runner top on both sides; check for proper seam pressing and trim all loose threads.

2. Sandwich batting between the stitched top and the backing piece; pin or baste layers together to hold. Quilt as desired by hand or machine. *Note: The runner shown was machine-quilted in the ditch of seams and with a motif over each four-block unit.*

3. When quilting is complete, trim batting and backing fabric even with raw edges of runner top.

4. Join binding strips on short ends with diagonal seams as shown in Figure 4 to make one long strip; trim seams to ¼" and press seams open.

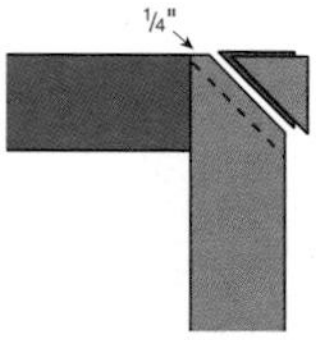

Figure 4

5. Fold the binding strip with wrong sides together along length; press.

6. Sew binding to runner edges, mitering corners and overlapping ends. Fold binding to the back side and stitch in place to finish. ❖

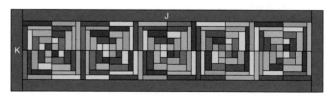

Chevron Tiles
Placement Diagram 81" x 21"

Diamond Holiday

Making Lone Star blocks is a wonderful way to use a variety of sizes of string scraps. Choose a color palette or use a lot of different-color scraps. Either method results in a striking quilt.

Project Note

Refer to Strings & Things introduction on page 2 for preparation of strings and general foundation-piecing instructions.

Project Specifications

Skill Level: Intermediate
Quilt Size: 40¼" x 40¼"

Materials

- Assorted bright red and green strings at least 9½" long by 1"–3½" wide, either straight or angled
- ¾ yard bright red tonal
- 1 yard white-with-gold mini dot
- 1⅜ yards white muslin (or use paper for foundations)
- Batting 48" x 48"
- Backing 48" x 48"
- Neutral-color all-purpose thread
- White, red and green quilting thread
- Water-soluble marking pen
- Template material
- Basic sewing tools and supplies

Cutting

1. Prepare a template for the A pattern using the pattern given; cut as directed to make foundation pieces.

2. Transfer joining dots from the template corners to the wrong side of each foundation piece.

3. Cut one 10¼" by fabric width strip white-with-gold mini dot; subcut strip into four 10" B squares.

4. Cut one 15" by fabric width strip white-with-gold mini dot; subcut strip into one 15" square. Cut the square on both diagonals to make four C triangles.

5. Cut two 1½" x 33¾" D strips and two 1½" x 35¾" E strips white-with-gold mini-dot.

6. Cut two 3" x 35¾" F strips and two 3" x 40¾" G strips bright red tonal

7. Cut four 2½" by fabric width strips bright red tonal for binding.

Completing the String Star Diamonds

1. Select and pin a green string right side up across the widest part of an A foundation piece as shown in Figure 1.

Figure 1

2. Position and pin a second green string right sides together and raw edges even with the pinned string; stitch through all layers as shown in Figure 2. **Note:** *Strings will extend beyond the A foundation piece.*

Figure 2

3. Press the top string to the right side as shown in Figure 3.

Figure 3

4. Turn the A foundation over and trim excess string length even with the foundation edges as shown in Figure 4. ***Note:*** *Save these trimmed ends to use again on shorter areas of the foundation. If your strings are already short, you may wait to trim all edges when the A foundation piece has been completely covered as shown in Figure 5.*

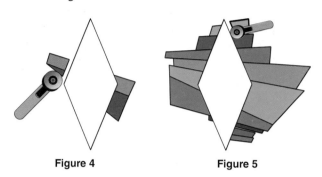

| Figure 4 | Figure 5 |

5. Turn the A foundation piece right side up; pin and stitch another string right sides together with the previously stitched string as shown in Figure 6; press and trim as in steps 3 and 4.

Figure 6

6. Continue to add strings and trim edges to fill the A foundation piece as shown in Figure 7.

Figure 7

7. Repeat steps 1–6 with green strings to complete a total of four green A diamonds and with red strings to complete a total of four red A diamonds.

Completing the Star Center

1. Select one each red and green A diamond. Match and pin edges of the two pieces together at the joining dots as shown in Figure 8.

Figure 8

2. Stitch the two pinned A pieces together between the joining dots to make an A section, backstitching at each end; press seam to the left.

Tips & Techniques

Backstitching set-in seams is a must, but be careful! Do not backstitch beyond the joining dots at the outside and inside points. To avoid excess thread build-up at the joining dots, begin sewing with the joining dot ¼" in front of the needle as shown in Figure 9.

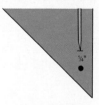

Figure 9

Stitch to the dot and, with the needle down, pivot work 180 degrees and continue stitching to the opposite joining dot as shown in Figure 10. Leave needle down and pivot 180 degrees again; stitch over seam ¼" to secure.

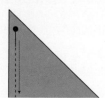

Figure 10

3. Repeat steps 1 and 2 to make a total of four A sections.

4. Mark joining dots at the ¼" seam-allowance intersections on the wrong side of each B square and C triangle as shown in Figure 11.

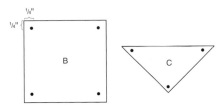

Figure 11

5. Match the dots of a joined A section to the dots on a B square as shown in Figure 12.

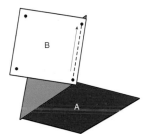

Figure 12

6. Starting at the inside angle of the pinned unit, stitch in the direction of the arrow from the marked dots to the outer edge referring to Figure 12; repeat on the second edge, stitching from the inside to the outside edge, referring to Figure 13.

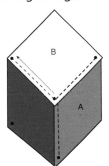

Figure 13

7. Press seams toward the B square to complete one corner unit.

8. Repeat steps 5–7 with remaining A sections and B squares to make a total of four corner units.

9. Join two of the corner units between joining dots as in step 2 to complete a half-star unit as shown in Figure 14; press seams in the same direction as other seams. Repeat to make a second half unit.

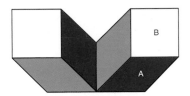

Figure 14

10. Join the half units, stitching from joining dot to joining dot, leaving the center seams unstitched as shown in Figure 15; press seams in the same direction as other seams and the center seams in a swirl as shown in Figure 16.

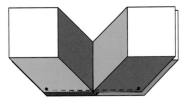

Figure 15

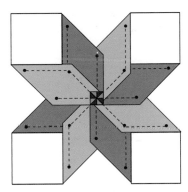

Figure 16

11. Insert and stitch C triangles between star points as for B squares and referring to Figure 17 to complete the pieced center; press seams toward C triangles.

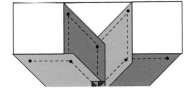

Figure 17

12. Sew D strips to opposite sides and E strips to the top and bottom of the pieced center; press seams toward D and E strips.

13. Sew F strips to opposite sides and G strips to the top and bottom of the pieced center to complete the pieced top; press seams toward F and G strips.

House of White Birches, Berne, Indiana 46711 Clotilde.com

Finishing

1. Press quilt top on both sides; check for proper seam pressing and trim all loose threads.

2. Sandwich batting between the stitched top and the backing piece; pin or baste layers together to hold. Quilt as desired by hand or machine.

3. When quilting is complete, trim batting and backing fabric even with raw edges of quilt top.

4. Join binding strips on short ends with diagonal seams as shown in Figure 18 to make one long strip; trim seams to ¼" and press seams open.

Figure 18

5. Fold the binding strip with wrong sides together along length; press.

6. Sew binding to quilt edges, mitering corners and overlapping ends. Fold binding to the back side and stitch in place to finish. ❖

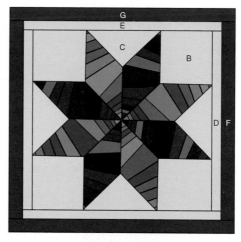

Diamond Holiday
Placement Diagram 40¼" x 40¼"

This design is equally striking as a complete scrap bag project.

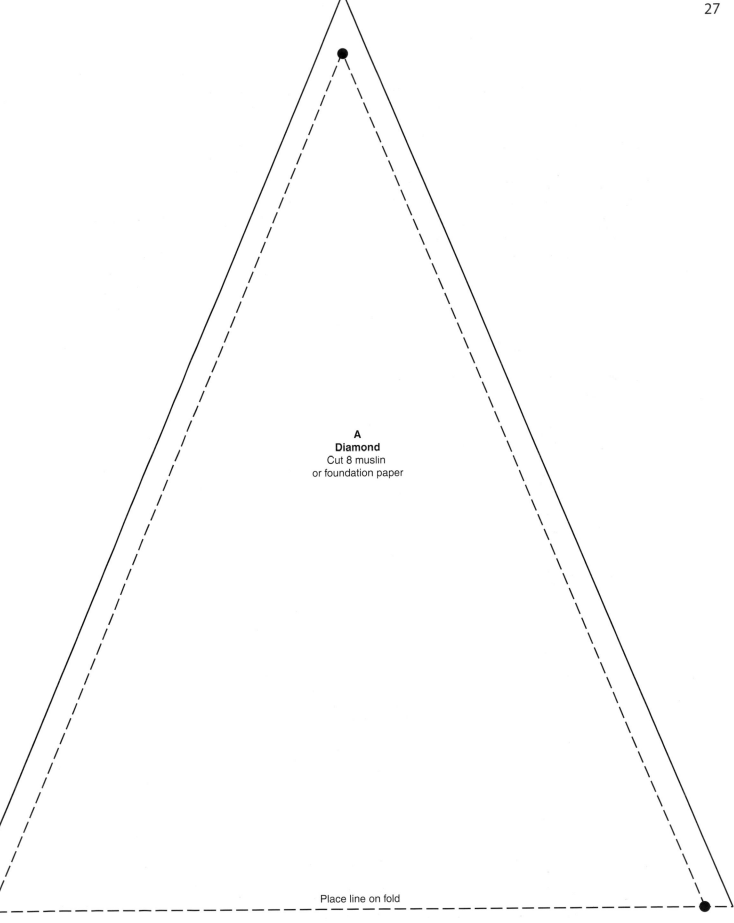

A
Diamond
Cut 8 muslin
or foundation paper

Place line on fold

House of White Birches, Berne, Indiana 46711   Clotilde.com

Play Ball!

Children will fall in love with this bright and colorful quilt! You will have just as much fun making it as you will giving it to them!

Project Specifications
Skill Level: Beginner
Quilt Size: 50" x 57"
Block Size: 7" x 7"
Number of Blocks: 21

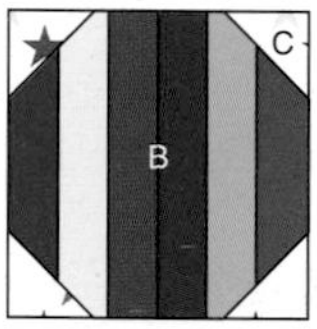

String Snowball
7" x 7" Block
Make 21

Materials
- Bright-color fabric strings to coordinate with multicolored stars print
- ¾ yard green mini dot
- ¾ yard bright green mottled
- 1⅝ yards multicolored stars print
- Batting 58" x 65"
- Backing 58" x 65"
- Neutral-color all-purpose thread
- Quilting thread
- 1 package 8½" x 11" foundation paper
- Basic sewing tools and supplies

Cutting
1. Draw a 7½" x 7½" square on one of the foundation papers. Draw a vertical line through the center to divide the square in half. Make 20 more copies of the square on foundation paper using a copy machine or by hand-tracing the square to make a total of 21 foundation squares; trim to make squares, leaving a margin beyond the line for trimming later. Set aside.

2. Prepare the bright-color strings referring to the Strings & Things introduction on page 2.

3. Cut five 1½" by fabric width D/E strips bright green mottled.

4. Cut six 2½" by fabric width strips bright green mottled for binding.

5. Cut six 3½" by fabric width F/G strips green mini dot.

6. Cut five 7½" by fabric width strips multicolored stars print; subcut strips into (21) 7½" A setting squares.

7. Cut six 2½" by fabric width strips multicolored stars print; subcut strips into (84) 2½" C squares.

Completing the String Snowball Blocks
1. Position a string right side up along the vertical line marked on the foundation square as shown in Figure 1.

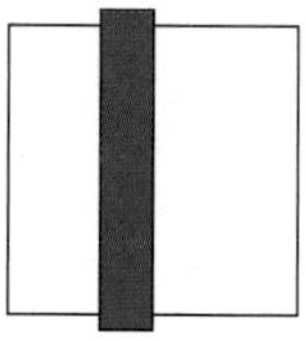

Figure 1

2. Place and pin a second string right sides together with the first string, matching one raw edge as shown in Figure 2.

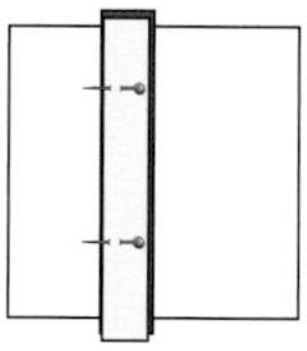

Figure 2

3. Set machine to stitch 18–20 stitches per inch; sew along matching raw edges of strips. Open and press as shown in Figure 3. *Note: A shorter stitch length makes it easier to remove foundation paper later.*

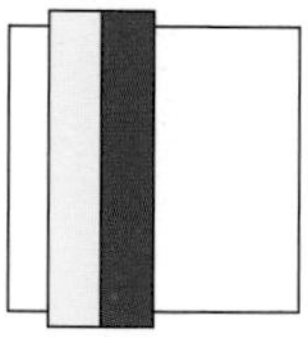

Figure 3

4. Position and stitch another string, right sides together, with the previous string and press as in step 3. *Note: Strings may be a uniform width as shown in the drawings or angled and varied widths as used in the sample quilt.*

5. Continue adding strings to cover the foundation square.

6. Turn the stitched square over with foundation square on top; trim along the marked outer line to make a 7½" x 7½" B string square as shown in Figure 4.

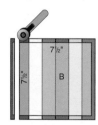

Figure 4

7. Repeat steps 1–6 to complete a total of 21 B string squares.

8. Draw a diagonal line from corner to corner on the wrong side of each C square.

9. Place a C square right sides together on one corner of a B string square and stitch on the marked line as shown in Figure 5. Repeat on each corner of the B string square.

Figure 5

10. Trim seams to ¼" and press C to the right side with seam toward C to complete one Snowball block referring to the block drawing on page 28.

11. Repeat steps 9 and 10 to complete a total of 21 String Snowball blocks.

12. Carefully remove the foundation paper from the String Snowball blocks and press flat.

Completing the Quilt Top

1. Select and join three String Snowball blocks and three A setting squares to make a row as shown in Figure 6; press seams toward A. Repeat to make a total of seven rows.

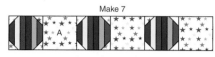

Figure 6

2. Join the rows, turning every other row to begin with the A setting blocks to complete the quilt center, referring to the Placement Diagram for positioning; press seams in one direction.

3. Join the D/E strips on short ends to make one long strip; press seams open. Subcut strip into two 49½" D strips and two 44½" E strips.

4. Sew D strips to opposite sides and E strips to the top and bottom of the quilt center; press seams toward D and E strips.

5. Repeat step 3 with F/G strips and subcut into two 51½" F strips and two 50½" G strips.

6. Sew F strips to opposite long sides and G strips to the top and bottom of the quilt center to complete the quilt top; press seams toward F and G strips.

Finishing

1. Press quilt top on both sides; check for proper seam pressing and trim all loose threads.

2. Sandwich batting between the stitched top and the backing piece; pin or baste layers together to hold. Quilt as desired by hand or machine.

3. When quilting is complete, trim batting and backing fabric even with raw edges of quilt top.

4. Join binding strips on short ends with diagonal seams as shown in Figure 7 to make one long strip; trim seams to ¼" and press seams open.

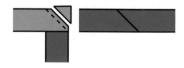

Figure 7

5. Fold the binding strip with wrong sides together along length; press.

6. Sew binding to quilt edges, mitering corners and overlapping ends. Fold binding to the back side and stitch in place to finish. ❖

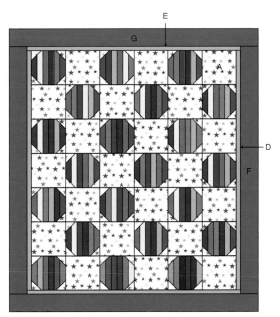

Play Ball
Placement Diagram 50" x 57"

House of White Birches, Berne, Indiana 46711   Clotilde.com

Summer Garden

Using an abundance of bright floral prints accented with leafy green prints brings the summer garden into any room in which this quilt resides.

Project Specifications
Skill Level: Beginner
Runner Size: 55" x 64"
Block Size: 6" x 6"
Number of Blocks: 30

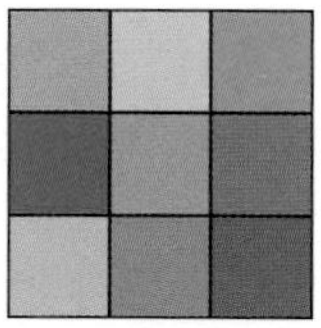

Nine-Patch
6" x 6" Block
Make 30

Materials
- 8 different green tonal fat quarters
- 12–15 different bright floral print fat quarters
- ⅔ yard black solid
- ⅞ yard medium green mottled
- Batting 63" x 72"
- Backing 63" x 72"
- Neutral-color all-purpose thread
- Coordinating green quilting thread
- Variegated pastel quilting thread
- Basic sewing tools and supplies

Cutting
1. Cut (12) 1½" x 18" C strings from each of the eight different green tonal fat quarters.

2. Cut (270) 2½" x 2½" A squares and (42) 3½" x 3½" B sashing squares from the 12–15 different bright floral print fat quarters.

3. Cut seven 2½" by fabric width strips black solid for binding.

4. Cut six 4" by fabric width D/E strips medium green mottled.

Completing the Nine-Patch Blocks
1. To complete one Nine-Patch block, select nine different A squares. **Note:** *The quilt will be brighter and more interesting if each square is a different fabric.*

2. Join three A squares to make the center row as shown in Figure 1; press seams toward the center A square.

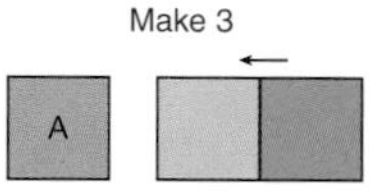

Make 3

Figure 1

3. Repeat step 2 to make a top and bottom row; press seams away from the center A square.

4. Join the rows to complete one Nine-Patch block referring to Figure 2.

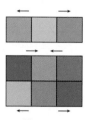

Figure 2

5. Repeat steps 1–4 to complete a total of 30 Nine-Patch blocks.

Completing the Sashing Units
1. Select six different C strings. Join the strings with right sides together along length to make a 6½" x 18" string set as shown in Figure 3; press seams in one direction.

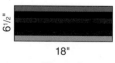

6½"

18"

Figure 3

2. Subcut the string set into five 3½" C sashing units as shown in Figure 4.

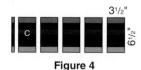

3½"

6½"

C

Figure 4

34

3. Repeat steps 1 and 2 to make a total of 16 string sets and subcut into a total of (71) 3½" x 6½" C sashing units.

Completing the Top

1. Select and join five Nine-Patch blocks and six C sashing units to complete a block row, beginning and ending with a C sashing unit as shown in Figure 5; press seams toward the C sashing units.

Make 6

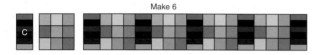

Figure 5

2. Repeat step 1 to make a total of six block rows.

3. Select and join six B sashing squares and five C sashing units to complete a sashing row, beginning and ending with B sashing squares as shown in Figure 6; press seams toward C sashing units.

Make 7

Figure 6

4. Repeat step 3 to complete a total of seven sashing rows.

5. Join the sashing rows with the block rows, beginning and ending with a sashing row, to complete the pieced center; press seams toward sashing rows.

6. Join D/E strips on short ends to make a long strip; press seams open. Subcut strip into two 57½" D strips and two 55½" E strips.

7. Sew D strips to opposite long sides and E strips to the top and bottom of the pieced center to complete the pieced top referring to the Placement Diagram; press seams toward D and E strips.

Finishing

1. Press quilt top on both sides; check for proper seam pressing and trim all loose threads.

2. Sandwich batting between the stitched top and the backing piece; pin or baste layers together to hold. Quilt as desired by hand or machine. ***Note:** The*

quilt shown was quilted with a leaf and vine design in the borders and a braid design in the sashing units using coordinating green thread. A variegated pastel thread was used to quilt a floral design in the Nine-Patch blocks and the B sashing squares.

3. When quilting is complete, trim batting and backing fabric even with raw edges of quilt top.

4. Join binding strips on short ends with diagonal seams as shown in Figure 7 to make one long strip; trim seams to ¼" and press seams open.

Figure 7

5. Fold the binding strip with wrong sides together along length; press.

6. Sew binding to quilt edges, mitering corners and overlapping ends. Fold binding to the back side and stitch in place to finish. ❖

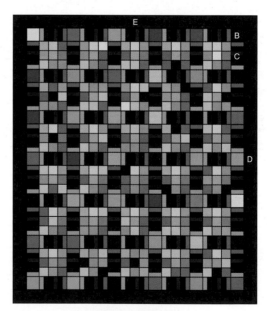

Summer Garden
Placement Diagram 55" x 64"

Royal Diamonds

Purple and gold are the colors of royalty. This design could be made using fabrics in other planned color arrangements or using a variety of scrap strings.

Project Specifications
- Skill Level: Intermediate
- Quilt Size: 88" x 96"
- Block Size: 8" x 8"
- Number of Blocks: 100

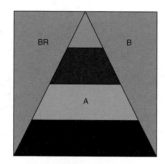

Diamond
8" x 8" Block
Make 100

Materials
- 13 fat quarters in assorted gold tonals and/or mottleds
- 2 yards cream mottled
- 4 yards total assorted purple tonals and/or mottleds
- Batting 96" x 104"
- Backing 96" x 104"
- Neutral-color all-purpose thread
- Quilting thread
- Template material
- Basic sewing tools and supplies

Cutting
1. Prepare templates for A and B pieces using patterns given.

2. Cut a total of (52) 2½" by fabric width A strings from purple tonals and/or mottleds.

3. Fold each gold fat quarter in half with right sides together to make a 9" x 21" rectangle; place the B template on a rectangle as shown in Figure 1 to cut B and BR pieces at the same time. ***Note:*** *You should*

be able to get eight sets of B/BR pieces from each fat quarter, again referring to Figure 1.

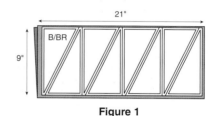

Figure 1

4. Repeat step 3 with remaining gold fabrics to cut a total of 100 each B and BR pieces. Keep pairs together as cut.

5. Cut eight 2½" by fabric width C strips cream mottled.

6. Cut nine 4½" by fabric width D strips cream mottled.

7. Cut a total of (10) 2½" by fabric width strips purple tonals for binding.

Completing the Blocks
1. Select four different A strings; join with right sides together along length to make an A string set. Press seams in one direction. Repeat to make a total of 13 A string sets.

2. Place the A template on a string set and cut as shown in Figure 2; continue to cut A pieces across the string set, again referring to Figure 2. ***Note:*** *You should be able to cut eight A pieces from each string set.*

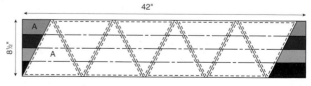

Figure 2

3. Repeat step 2 to cut a total of 100 A pieces.

4. Sew B to one long side of A as shown in Figure 3; press seam toward B.

Figure 3

5. Sew BR to opposite long side of A as in step 4 to complete one Diamond block referring to Figure 4; press seam toward BR.

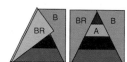

Figure 4

6. Repeat steps 4 and 5 to complete a total of 100 Diamond blocks.

Completing the Top

1. Select and join 10 Diamond blocks to make a row; press seams in one direction. Repeat to make a total of 10 rows.

2. Join two rows to make a block row as shown in Figure 5; press seam in one direction. Repeat with remaining rows to make a total of five block rows.

Make 5

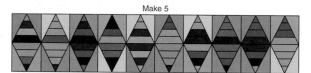

Figure 5

3. Join the C strips on short ends to make one long strip; press seams open. Subcut strip into four 80½" C sashing strips.

4. Join the block rows with the C sashing strips, beginning and ending with the block rows to complete the pieced center; press seams toward C sashing strips.

5. Join the D strips on short ends to make one long strip; press seams open. Subcut strips in four 88½" D strips.

6. Sew a D strip to opposite long sides and then to the top and bottom of the pieced center to complete the pieced top; press seams toward D strips.

Finishing

1. Press quilt top on both sides; check for proper seam pressing and trim all loose threads.

2. Sandwich batting between the stitched top and the backing piece; pin or baste layers together to hold. Quilt as desired by hand or machine.

3. When quilting is complete, trim batting and backing fabric even with raw edges of quilt top.

4. Join binding strips on short ends with diagonal seams as shown in Figure 6 to make one long strip; trim seams to ¼" and press seams open.

Figure 6

5. Fold the binding strip with wrong sides together along length; press.

6. Sew binding to quilt top edges, mitering corners and overlapping ends. Fold binding to the back side and stitch in place to finish. ❖

Royal Diamonds
Placement Diagram 88" x 96"

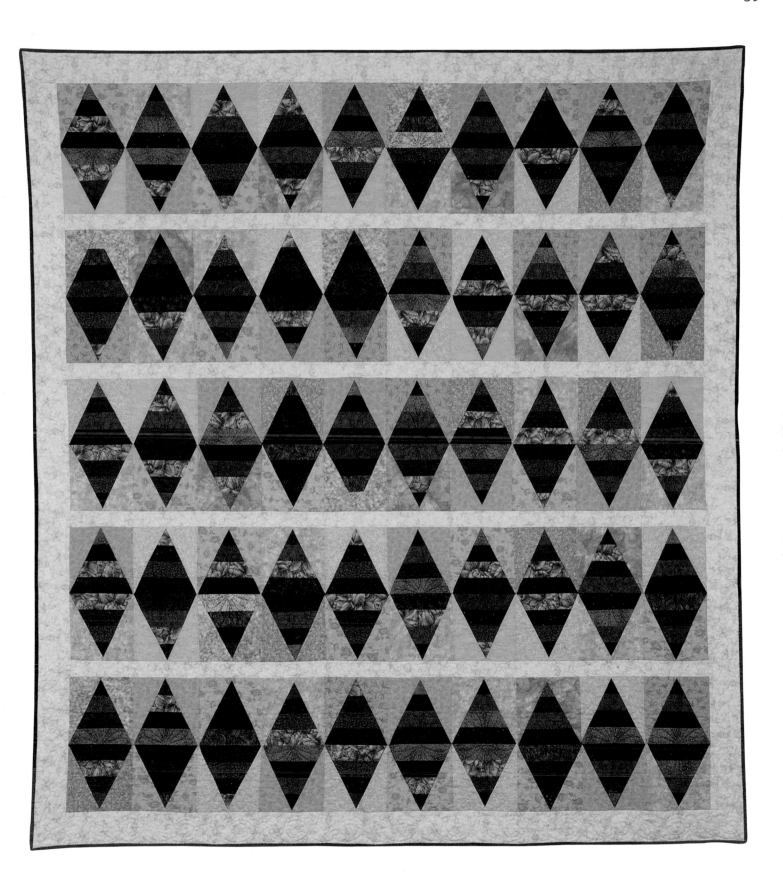

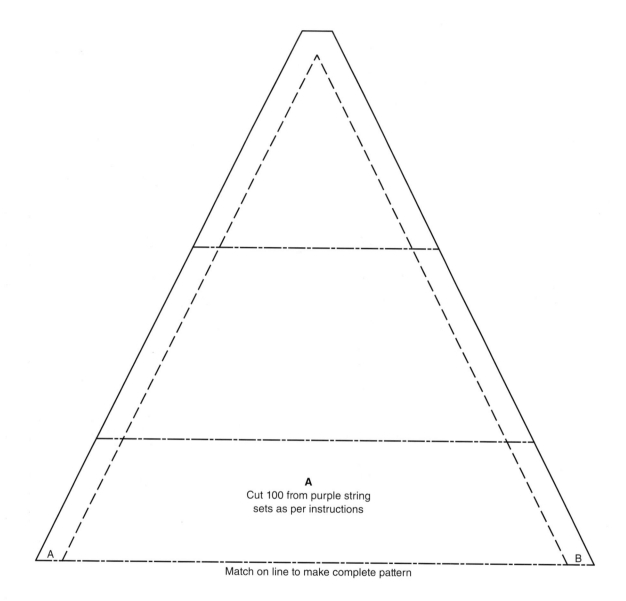

A
Cut 100 from purple string
sets as per instructions

Match on line to make complete pattern

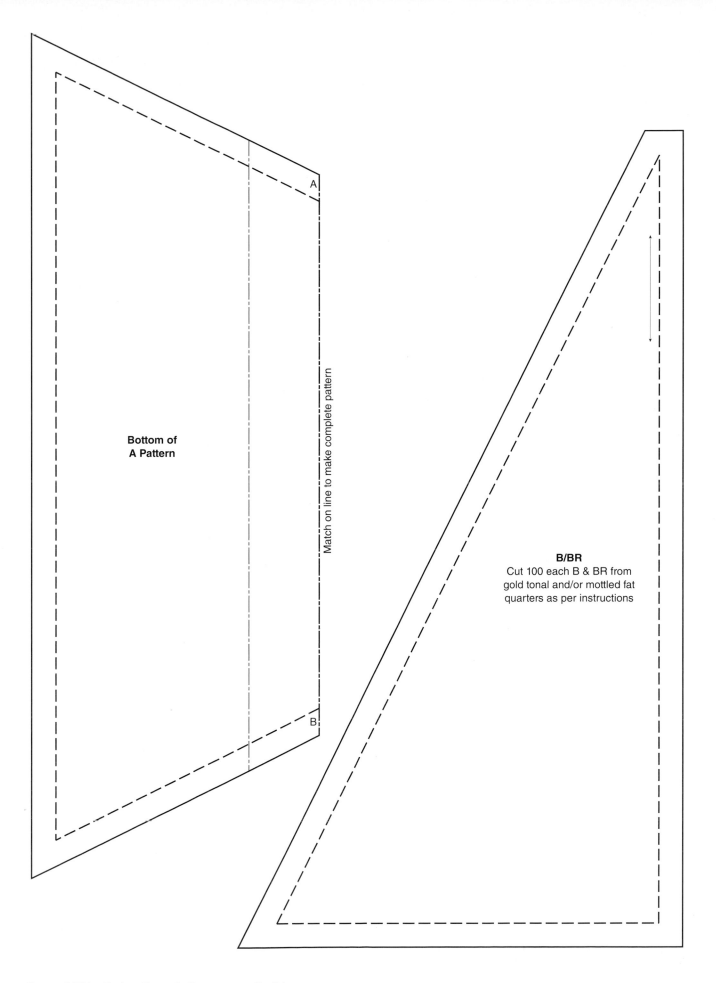

41

**Bottom of
A Pattern**

Match on line to make complete pattern

A

B

B/BR
Cut 100 each B & BR from
gold tonal and/or mottled fat
quarters as per instructions

Autumn Equinox

This is a classic string quilt. Choose autumn colors from a bundle of fat quarters and add fabrics from your stash.

Project Notes
If you were to join string strips and cut into 8" x 8" squares with the strings on the diagonal, you would end up with a block with all diagonal edges. Sewing the strips to a foundation of fabric, paper or other foundation material stabilizes those bias edges until they are stitched together with sashing strips in rows. If using paper, it is then removed. If using a fabric foundation, it remains as part of the quilt and adds a bit of weight to the finished quilt.

Project Specifications
- Skill Level: Beginner
- Quilt Size: 77" x 97"
- Block Size: 8" x 8"
- Number of Blocks: 63

Materials
- Assorted autumn-color strings including dark reds, oranges, golds and greens
- ½ yard gold tonal
- 2 yards cream tonal
- 2⅛ yards brown tonal
- 4 yards muslin or (63) 8½" x 8½" squares paper for foundations
- Batting 85" x 105"
- Backing 85" x 105"
- Neutral-color all-purpose thread
- Quilting thread
- Basic sewing tools and supplies

Cutting
1. Cut (16) 8½" by fabric width strips muslin; subcut strips into (63) 8½" squares for foundations. **Note:** *You may use paper instead of muslin for foundations. If using paper, it will have to be removed once the blocks are completed. If using muslin, it becomes part of the block and makes a heavier quilt.*

Strings
8" x 8" Block
Make 63

2. Cut seven 8½" by fabric width strips cream tonal; subcut strips into (110) 2½" A strips.

3. Cut three 2½" by fabric width strips brown tonal; subcut strips into (48) 2½" B squares.

4. Cut nine 4" by fabric width E/F strips brown tonal.

5. Cut nine 2¼" by fabric width strips brown tonal for binding.

6. Cut eight 1½" by fabric width C/D strips gold tonal.

7. Cut the assorted autumn-color fabrics into 1½"–2¾" by fabric width strings for piecing blocks.

Completing the Blocks
1. Place a string right side up on the diagonal of an 8½" x 8½" muslin or paper foundation as shown in Figure 1.

Figure 1

2. Place another string right sides together on top of the previously placed string, matching raw edges; stitch along matched edges of string using a ¼" seam allowance as shown in Figure 2.

Figure 2

3. Press the top string to the right side.

4. Turn the square over and trim excess string even with the edge of the foundation square as shown in Figure 3. ***Note:*** *If you prefer, you may trim excess string a bit larger than the foundation and leave the exact trimming until all strings have been added to the square as shown in Figure 4.*

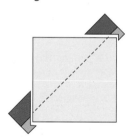

Figure 3

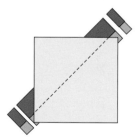

Figure 4

5. Repeat steps 2–4 to add strings to cover the entire foundation as shown in Figure 5.

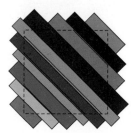

Figure 5

6. If you elected not to exact trim strings in previous steps, turn the foundation over and trim all edges even with the foundation square to complete one Strings block as shown in Figure 6.

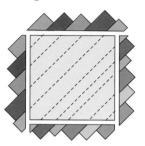

Figure 6

7. Repeat steps 1–6 to complete a total of 63 Strings blocks.

Completing the Top

1. Select seven Strings blocks and six A sashing strips. Join the blocks with A to make a block row, alternating the diagonal direction of the blocks, and beginning and ending the row with a block as shown in Figure 7; press seams toward the A sashing strips.

Make 9

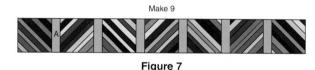

Figure 7

2. Repeat step 1 to complete a total of nine block rows.

3. Select and join seven A sashing strips and six B squares to make a sashing row, beginning and ending the row with an A sashing strip as shown in Figure 8; press seams toward the B sashing squares.

B   A

Figure 8

4. Repeat step 3 to complete a total of eight sashing rows.

5. Arrange and join the block rows (turning every other row referring to the Placement Diagram) with the sashing rows, beginning and ending with a block row to complete the pieced center; press seams toward sashing rows.

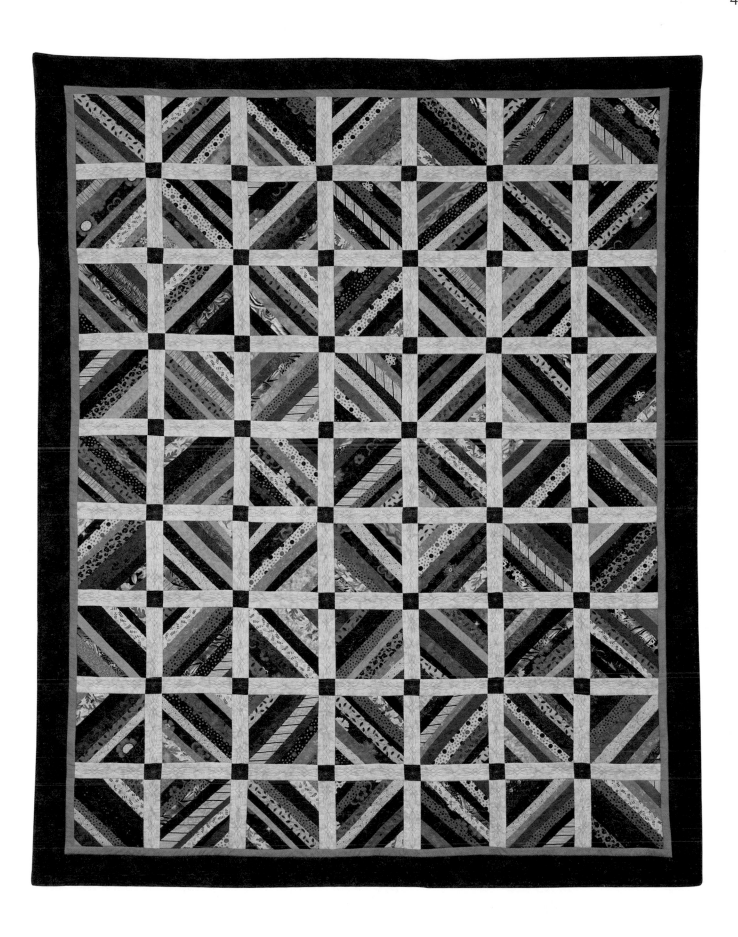

6. Join the C/D strips on short ends to make one long strip; press seams open. Subcut strip into two 88½" C strips and two 70½" D strips.

7. Sew C strips to opposite long sides and D strips to the top and bottom of the pieced center; press seams toward C and D strips. *Note: If using paper foundation squares, remove paper from the back of the blocks at this time; press the pieced top.*

8. Join the E/F strips on short ends to make one long strip; press seams open. Subcut strip into two 90½" E strips and two 77½" F strips.

9. Sew E strips to opposite long sides and F strips to the top and bottom of the pieced center to complete the quilt top; press seams toward E and F strips.

Finishing

1. Press quilt top on both sides; check for proper seam pressing and trim all loose threads.

2. Sandwich batting between the stitched top and the backing piece; pin or baste layers together to hold. Quilt as desired by hand or machine.

3. When quilting is complete, trim batting and backing fabric even with raw edges of quilt top.

4. Join binding strips on short ends with diagonal seams as shown in Figure 9 to make one long strip; trim seams to ¼" and press seams open.

Figure 9

5. Fold the binding strip with wrong sides together along length; press.

6. Sew binding to quilt top edges, mitering corners and overlapping ends. Fold binding to the back side and stitch in place to finish. ❖

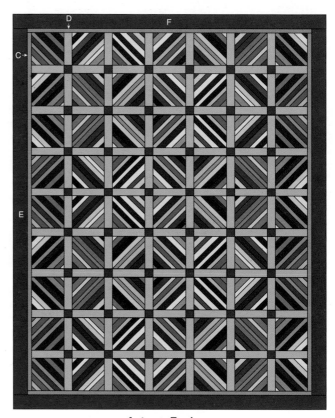

Autumn Equinox
Placement Diagram 77" x 97"

METRIC CONVERSION CHARTS

Metric Conversions

Canada/U.S. Measurement		Multiplied by		Metric Measurement
yards	x	.9144	=	metres (m)
yards	x	91.44	=	centimetres (cm)
inches	x	2.54	=	centimetres (cm)
inches	x	25.40	=	millimetres (mm)
inches	x	.0254	=	metres (m)

Canada/U.S. Measurement		Multiplied by		Metric Measurement
centimetres	x	.3937	=	inches
metres	x	1.0936	=	yards

Standard Equivalents

Canada/U.S. Measurement		Metric Measurement		
⅛ inch	=	3.20 mm	=	0.32 cm
¼ inch	=	6.35 mm	=	0.635 cm
⅜ inch	=	9.50 mm	=	0.95 cm
½ inch	=	12.70 mm	=	1.27 cm
⅝ inch	=	15.90 mm	=	1.59 cm
¾ inch	=	19.10 mm	=	1.91 cm
⅞ inch	=	22.20 mm	=	2.22 cm
1 inches	=	25.40 mm	=	2.54 cm
⅛ yard	=	11.43 cm	=	0.11 m
¼ yard	=	22.86 cm	=	0.23 m
⅜ yard	=	34.29 cm	=	0.34 m
½ yard	=	45.72 cm	=	0.46 m
⅝ yard	=	57.15 cm	=	0.57 m
¾ yard	=	68.58 cm	=	0.69 m
⅞ yard	=	80.00 cm	=	0.80 m
1 yard	=	91.44 cm	=	0.91 m
1⅛ yards	=	102.87 cm	=	1.03 m
1¼ yards	=	114.30 cm	=	1.14 m

Canada/U.S. Measurement		Metric Measurement		
1⅜ yards	=	125.73 cm	=	1.26 m
1½ yards	=	137.16 cm	=	1.37 m
1⅝ yards	=	148.59 cm	=	1.49 m
1¾ yards	=	160.02 cm	=	1.60 m
1⅞ yards	=	171.44 cm	=	1.71 m
2 yards	=	182.88 cm	=	1.83 m
2⅛ yards	=	194.31 cm	=	1.94 m
2¼ yards	=	205.74 cm	=	2.06 m
2⅜ yards	=	217.17 cm	=	2.17 m
2½ yards	=	228.60 cm	=	2.29 m
2⅝ yards	=	240.03 cm	=	2.40 m
2¾ yards	=	251.46 cm	=	2.51 m
2⅞ yards	=	262.88 cm	=	2.63 m
3 yards	=	274.32 cm	=	2.74 m
3⅛ yards	=	285.75 cm	=	2.86 m
3¼ yards	=	297.18 cm	=	2.97 m
3⅜ yards	=	308.61 cm	=	3.09 m
3½ yards	=	320.04 cm	=	3.20 m
3⅝ yards	=	331.47 cm	=	3.31 m
3¾ yards	=	342.90 cm	=	3.43 m
3⅞ yards	=	354.32 cm	=	3.54 m
4 yards	=	365.76 cm	=	3.66 m
4⅛ yards	=	377.19 cm	=	3.77 m
4¼ yards	=	388.62 cm	=	3.89 m
4⅜ yards	=	400.05 cm	=	4.00 m
4½ yards	=	411.48 cm	=	4.11 m
4⅝ yards	=	422.91 cm	=	4.23 m
4¾ yards	=	434.34 cm	=	4.34 m
4⅞ yards	=	445.76 cm	=	4.46 m
5 yards	=	457.20 cm	=	4.57 m

House of White Birches, Berne, Indiana 46711   Clotilde.com

Photo Index

8

5

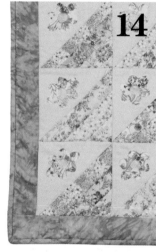

14

18

23

28

32

36

43